KT-513-453

On The Trail Of The CELTS

The CELTS In Britain

Peter Chrisp

W
FRANKLIN WATTS
LONDON•SYDNEY

© 1999 Franklin Watts
First published in Great Britain by
Franklin Watts
96 Leonard Street
London EC2A 4XD

Franklin Watts Australia
14 Mars Road
Lane Cove
NSW 2006
Australia

ISBN 0 7496 3227 5 (hbk)
ISBN 0 7496 3819 2 (pbk)

Dewey Decimal Classification 941.01
A CIP record for this book is
available from the British Library

Printed at Oriental Press, Dubai, U.A.E.

Planning and production by Discovery Books Ltd
Editor: Helena Attlee
Design: Simon Borrough
Consultant: Tim Copeland
Artwork: Stuart Carter, Mike Lacey,
Stefan Chabluk

Photographs: All pictures are by Alex Ramsay
except: Lesley & Roy Adkins Picture Library:
pages 11 (bottom), 19 (bottom); The British
Museum: pages 5 (both), 14 (left), 17 (bottom), 23,
26 (top); Colchester Archaeological Trust: 24-25
(all); Colchester Museums: page 21 (bottom);
Crown Copyright: reproduced by permission of
Historic Scotland: 12-13, 13, 17 (top); The Scottish
Crannog Centre/Barry Andrian: 14-15 (main
picture), 15; The Stock Market: page 27.

CONTENTS

WHO WERE THE CELTS?

Two thousand years ago, Britain was home to a people called the Celts. There were Celts in many parts of Europe.

The Celts belonged to many different tribes with different names. We use the name 'Celt' as a label to describe people who spoke similar languages and followed the same way of life.

As far as we know, the Celts did not write books. To find out how they lived, we rely on the writings of other people, especially the Romans. The Romans visited and then invaded Britain, and they wrote descriptions of what they saw. The problem with Roman writers is that they looked down on the Celts as backward savages, so their accounts were not always accurate. Luckily, we have another way of finding out about Celtic life in Britain, through archaeology.

Thanks to the Romans, we know the names of the main Celtic tribes of Britain.

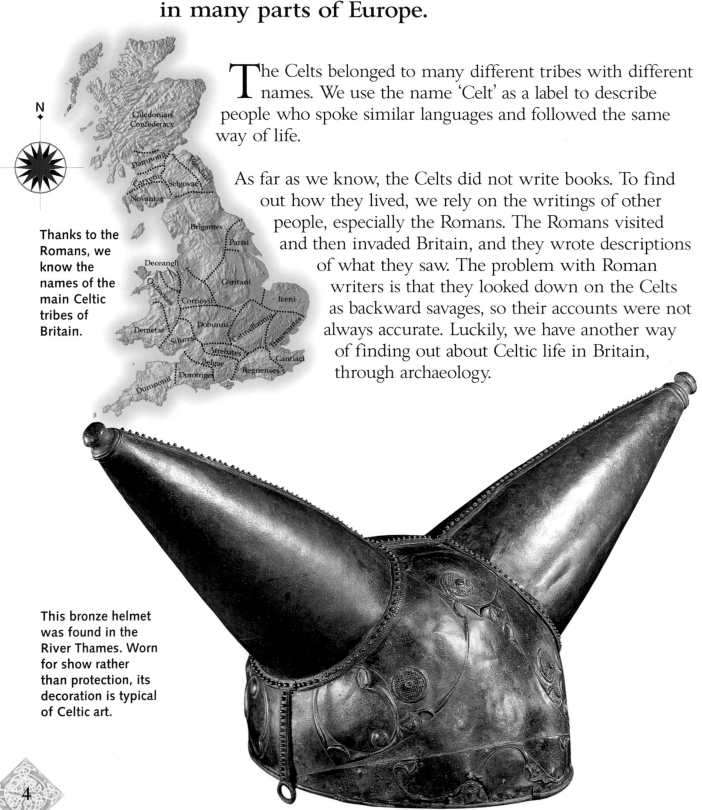

This bronze helmet was found in the River Thames. Worn for show rather than protection, its decoration is typical of Celtic art.

CELTIC CLOTHES

The Celts wore striking clothing, with shirts and trousers dyed in various colours. They used brooches or belts to secure their clothes. Diodorus of Sicily was a Greek who lived in the Roman Empire. He described the Celts in these words: 'Some of the men shave the beard, but let the moustache grow until it covers the mouth. When they are eating, they often get their food tangled in their moustaches!'

Archaeology is the study of things left behind by people who lived in the past. The Celts of Britain have left all sorts of evidence for archaeologists to study.

There are Celtic hill-forts, chalk pictures on hillsides and the remains of buildings. There are also many chance finds of beautiful Celtic metalwork, from rivers and fields.

GAMES

Rich Celts relaxed by playing board games. These glass gaming pieces were found in a chieftain's grave at Welwyn. They were probably used in games like draughts.

The Celts loved jewellery with inlaid patterns. This brooch was used to fasten a cloak.

CELTIC DEFENCES

The most spectacular remains of the Celts are the hundreds of hill-forts that they built in many parts of Britain.

Although they are called 'forts', they were more like defended villages, or small towns. Inside, there were often dozens of round-houses (see page 9).

Maiden Castle in Dorset is one of the biggest hill-forts in Britain. It has massive defences made up of a series of tall earth banks and deep ditches. Archaeologists have discovered that the banks originally measured 25m from top to bottom. The ditches were even deeper than they are today.

The fact that people needed to build such strong defences shows us that warfare between the tribes was common. We are also told

Imagine trying to run up the banks at Maiden Castle with a hail of pebbles pouring down on you. This fort must have been very difficult for enemies to storm.

Key
· Hill-fort
• 2-5 Hill-forts
● 5-10 Hill-forts

N

this by Strabo, a Roman writer who said of the Celts, 'the whole race is war-mad, high-spirited and quick for battle.'

Archaeologists also discovered a pit holding more than 20 thousand pebbles at Maiden Castle. All the pebbles had been brought up to the castle from the seashore and so they must have had a special use. They were probably used as ammunition to fire out of a leather sling at attackers.

This picture shows what the whole of Maiden Castle looks like.

At the hill-forts of Bredon Hill in Worcestershire and Stanwick in Yorkshire, archaeologists have found collections of human skulls. They may have been collected as trophies by the winners of a battle.

WOODEN DWELLINGS

In Celtic times, the south and east of Britain was thickly wooded. The Celts of the lowlands used wood to build their homes.

Wooden buildings rot. Usually the only traces of Celtic houses are the holes left by the wooden posts that held them up. By studying the size and position of the post-holes, archaeologists can imagine what the building once looked like.

Here you can see the posts that held up the enormous sloping roof.

The roof was thatched with straw, from wheat grown on the farm.

In 1960, a Celtic house was discovered in Wiltshire, at Longbridge Deverill Cow Down. The house had burned down, leaving the blackened bases of the posts visible in the ground. The circular building was 15m in diameter, which makes it the biggest Celtic house ever found in Britain. Its size suggests that it must have been the home of someone rich and powerful.

At Butser Ancient Farm, in Hampshire, they have rebuilt the Longbridge round-house, using the evidence that they found on the original site. The outer wall is made of wattle which is plastered with mud, to keep the wind out. The tall sloping roof has been thatched. It took 15 tonnes of straw to cover it.

◀ This is a modern reconstruction of a Celtic round-house, at Butser Ancient Farm in Hampshire.

COOKING
The Celts cooked their meals on an open fire in the centre of their homes. Archaeologists have found a lot of evidence of Celtic cooking, including hearths, animal bones, burnt grains, and bronze and iron cooking pots still coated with soot from the fire.

The hearth at Butser.

STONE SETTLEMENTS

On high ground or moorland there are few trees. Celts living in these places built their homes from stone rather than wood.

Here you can see one of the rooms in a house at Chysauster, with the courtyard behind.

At Chysauster, on the windswept moors of Cornwall, you can visit a Celtic village with nine stone houses. Although the roofs of the houses have disappeared, the walls are still between two and three metres high.

Each house has a central courtyard, with rooms off it, surrounded by a massive wall. The thick wall provided shelter and protection for the people and their animals. A long entrance passage faces east or north-east, away from the usual direction of the wind.

In the middle of some rooms, there is a stone with a hole in it. This was a socket for the pole which held up the roof. Each room was like a separate hut with its own tall roof, thatched with straw or covered with grassy turves. The family probably lived in one room, while other rooms were used for the farm animals and for storing food.

Ingleborough was the site of several stone houses. Unlike wood, stones do not rot away. They provide vital clues for archaeologists.

Ingleborough in Yorkshire is the highest hill-fort in the country. There are no trees in this area, but there was plenty of stone that the Celts could use to make houses. The remains of twenty round-houses have been found. The wood for making roofs had to be carried all the way up from the valley below.

SPINNING WOOL
Celtic clothes were usually made from wool. In Celtic houses, archaeologists often find small round weights, made of bone, clay or stone, with a hole through the middle. These are 'spindle whorls' and they were used for spinning wool. Each whorl was fastened to the end of a stick, called a spindle. Wool was tied to the spindle, which was then spun in the air, twisting it into thread.

This woman is on a reconstructed Celtic site. She is dressed as a Celt, and has learned to spin wool using a weighted spindle.

CELTIC TOWERS

In the north of Scotland and on the Scottish islands, people built stone tower-houses for themselves called brochs.

This broch is at Dun Carloway on the island of Lewis. You can see that it has an inner and an outer wall, with a space in between. There are stairs inside the space, leading to upper levels. Inside the broch, a ledge sticks out of the wall about 2m above the ground. This may have supported an upper floor or a walkway.

Many brochs have fallen into ruin because local people carried the stones away to build their homes.

The best preserved broch is on Mousa, a tiny island off Shetland. It is 13m high with curving sides - a sturdy shape. With only one little door as an outside opening, the people who lived here were well-protected against attack. The houses must have been very dark inside.

Archaeologists can only guess at how the brochs were used. Some believe that the ground floor was used for storage and for sheltering animals in winter. They think that people lived on the upper floor. No one can be sure of the truth and there is still a lot of disagreement among archaeologists about the way that the Scottish Celts lived in their brochs.

The Mousa broch is one of the best preserved ancient buildings in Britain.

Brochs were often built near water. The idea of broch building was probably spread by people travelling in boats. This suggests that it was much easier to travel by sea than by land in Celtic times.

Key
• Broch
• 2-5 Brochs

N

This map shows us that many brochs are found close to the sea.

LIVING ON WATER

Brochs were not the only strange structures lived in by the Celts. In the Scottish Highlands, some people lived on artificial islands called crannogs.

There were once 18 crannogs on Loch Tay. Now they have all sunk below the water or become overgrown with plants. Archaeologists have spent many years finding the crannogs and studying them. They often had to work under the water, which was very difficult and uncomfortable.

By studying the evidence, archaeologists have learned that the crannogs were made by driving wooden posts into the bottom of the loch. Rocks, branches and turf were dropped between the posts. These formed a solid base for the crannog.

This is a modern reconstruction of a crannog on Loch Tay.

14

Between 1995 and 1996, a team of archaeologists built their own crannog on the loch. They spent a year building the base. Then they built a big round-house on top.

Archaeologists wanted to find out why the Celts went to so much trouble to live on water. One possible reason was for protection from attack, either by other people or by wild animals. Wolves and bears still roamed Britain in those days. Also, the crannog house stands out against the water. The people who lived in such a place may have wanted to show their neighbours that they were rich and important.

▲ The archaeologists have filled the crannog with reconstructions of household items, including a loom for spinning wool, on the right.

Wood can last for thousands of years under water. Many wooden objects were found in Loch Tay. The biggest was a boat which had been hollowed out of an oak tree. Grains, seeds, nuts and animal droppings were also found. Archaeologists have been able to use this evidence to find out about the food the Celts ate and the kinds of animals they kept. They even found a broken butter dish with the greasy remains of butter in it.

15

MYSTERIOUS TUNNELS

In Cornwall, stone-lined tunnels called 'fogous' are often found beside Celtic houses. They are also found in Scotland, where they are known as 'souterrains'.

This fogou at Boleigh in Cornwall is 12m long and 1.5m wide, with a small L-shaped side-passage. People went to a lot of trouble to build it, so it must have had an important use. Unfortunately, nobody knows what that use was. It is too dark and cramped to live in.

One idea is that the fogou was a place to hide if the settlement was attacked, but the entrance is very easy to find. Anyone hiding inside would have been trapped by their enemies.

You have to bend double to get through the cramped entrance to the Boleigh fogou.

This is a Scottish stone tunnel, or souterrain, on Orkney.

Some people think that fogous were built for religious reasons. The Celts believed in gods who lived beneath the earth. Perhaps the fogou was a way of getting closer to the gods.

Many archaeologists believe that fogous were used for storage. A cool, dark tunnel would have been a good place to keep milk, cheese and grain.

TIN

The people who lived at Boleigh were farmers, like most Celts, but they had another way to make a living. They traded in tin, which they found lying in the local streams. Tin was valuable because it is only found in small areas of Britain. It was mixed with copper to make bronze, the metal used by the Celts for helmets, shields, mirrors and other decorative work.

A decorated bronze mirror. The other side was polished until it reflected the owner's face.

FARMING

Most Celtic people lived by farming. They grew their crops in small square fields, ploughing them using teams of oxen.

Like Celtic fields, the fields at Butser are small and square.

Butser Ancient Farm in Hampshire is a working farm, where crops are still being grown using Celtic methods. They grow wheat, barley, oats, peas and beans. We know that these were grown by the Celts because of finds of burnt grains and seeds in archaeological digs.

◄ The Butser farmers use reconstructions of Celtic farming tools, such as this wooden plough.

Celtic farming has left traces all over the British countryside. On many hillsides, you can see earth banks, called 'lynchets'. They were made by Celtic farmers, ploughing the fields. Gradually, soil slipped down the hillside to the lower edge of the field, where it is built up forming the bank.

On the chalk downlands, archaeologists have dug under Celtic fields and found signs of Celtic ploughing. The chalk surface, just beneath the soil, was scored with lines, scratched by ploughs. The lines were in a criss-cross pattern, showing that the farmers ploughed each field twice. They did this because they only had a light plough. Unlike the heavier plough used by later farmers, it could not turn over the soil, it just scratched a furrow. The Celts had to plough twice to break up the soil properly.

POTTERY
In the first century BC, the Celts learned to make pots by spinning them on a wheel – an idea brought across the sea from mainland Europe. We know this because they began to produce curved pots with a smooth finish. Previously, all pots had been shaped by hand. This did not produce as fine a finish.

This Celtic pot was made on a wheel. It was found in Somerset.

Chalk Figures

Chalk lies just beneath the green turf on many British hills. The Celts used the chalk to make huge white pictures on the hillsides.

One of the best chalk pictures lies just below a Celtic hill-fort, at Uffington in Oxfordshire. It shows a great white horse, 111m long. Seen from a distance, the horse looks as if it is galloping across the hills.

At Cerne Abbas in Dorset, you can see a chalk picture of a giant holding a club. At Wilmington in Sussex, there is a man holding two long poles. Nobody knows who made these pictures, or why they did it. Perhaps they were a warning to people from other tribes to stay away. Perhaps they were made to please the gods.

▼ **This is how the Uffington White Horse looks from a distance.**

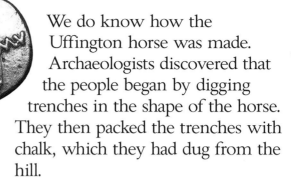

COINS

The horse was important to the Celts. They often put pictures of it on their gold coins. Another common image on Celtic coins is an ear of wheat. This shows how important farming was to the Celts.

▼ This is the head of the White Horse, with its eye in the centre.

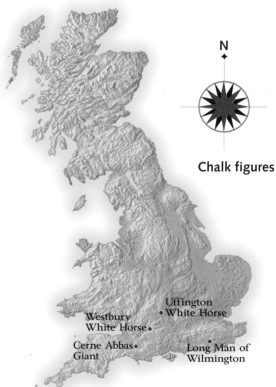

We do know how the Uffington horse was made. Archaeologists discovered that the people began by digging trenches in the shape of the horse. They then packed the trenches with chalk, which they had dug from the hill.

A new scientific method has been used to date the horse. It is called 'optical dating' and it tells us when sunlight last shone on buried soil. By testing soil from the trenches, the archaeologists discovered that the horse is at least 2,500 years old.

Chalk figures

Uffington
• White Horse

Westbury
White Horse •

Cerne Abbas •
Giant

Long Man of
Wilmington

Not all of the chalk figures in Britain are Celtic. Some of them may be Roman. The White Horse at Westbury was made in the eighteenth century.

CELTIC RELIGION

The Celts seem to have believed that many of their Gods lived beneath the water.

Celtic people thought that rivers, lakes and springs were holy places. Treasures found beneath the water were probably offerings to Celtic gods, made to win their help.

These strips of cloth are called 'clouties'. They were left at Craigie Well in Inverness.

In some parts of the countryside, people still leave offerings at holy wells and springs. They may believe that this will cure them of an illness or bring them good luck.

All over Britain, valuable pieces of Celtic bronzework have been discovered by accident, in rivers, lakes, bogs and springs.

When the tide is low, you can sometimes find amazing things in the River Thames as it flows through London. People have picked up beautiful Celtic metalwork lying in the Thames mud. Finds include swords, spear-heads, shields, a cauldron and a helmet. Much more metalwork has been discovered in the river as it flows through the countryside on its way to the city.

This bronze shield, decorated with red glass studs, was found in 1857 in the Thames at Battersea, London.

Craigie Well
St. Mary's Well, Culloden
Well of the Heads

N

Lady's Well
Coventina's Well

St. Gwenfaen's Well
St. Mary's Well
Holy Well
St. Anne's Well

St. Non's Well
Virtuous Well

St. Non's Well, Altarnun
St. Melor's Well

Ancient holy wells in Britain.

You can see several of the things that have been found on display in the British Museum and the Museum of London. There are so many of them that they cannot have been dropped into the river by accident. Celtic nobles may have wanted to show off their wealth by throwing some of it away.

23

BURYING THE DEAD

The Celts were often buried with their belongings. We can use these objects to build up a picture of their lives.

A collection of pottery found in the Warrior's Grave at Stanway.

At Stanway, in Essex, archaeologists have discovered a cemetery where wealthy Celts were buried. Their bodies were burned and the ashes placed in the earth with all sorts of goods, including pots, weapons, jewellery and gaming pieces.

This archaeologists is excavating a game board and counters that were found in the Doctor's Grave at Stanway.

The wealth of the grave-goods shows that these Celts were important people. They must have been nobles from the local tribe, the Trinovantes.

The Stanway burials show that the Celts believed in an afterlife, another world where they could go on living the same sort of life that they had lived on earth. Many of the goods had been deliberately broken. This was a way of sending them into the next world.

TRADE
Many of the goods buried at Stanway came across the sea from the Roman Empire. Roman writers tell us that their merchants sailed to Britain to buy wheat, slaves, tin and hunting dogs. In exchange, they supplied British nobles with wine, olive oil, precious glass like this bowl and metalwork.

►A Roman glass bowl, which belonged to one of the Celts buried at Stanway.

At Wetwang Slack, in Yorkshire, archaeologists dug up the bodies of two Celtic men and women, each with their own war chariot. Perhaps this was done so that they could ride in style into the next world.

▼ An iron spearhead found in the Warrior's Grave at Stanway. The wooden shaft had rotted away completely.

HUMAN SACRIFICE

According to Roman writers, the Celts killed people in special ways when they wanted to offer their bodies as gifts to the gods. Different kinds of death were chosen for different gods.

This is Lindow Moss, a peat bog near Manchester. In 1984, some peat diggers came across the body of a naked man in the bog. He was about 25 years old, 1.69m tall, with short hair and a beard, and neatly cut fingernails. The diggers called the police, thinking that they had found a recent murder victim.

The brown peat of Lindow Moss, where the body (right) was found. If you look carefully, you can see the cord used to strangle the dead man, still tied around his neck.

Since the late 1800s, modern Druids have been performing ceremonies at Stonehenge, which was wrongly believed to be a Druid temple. It is much older.

Peat, which is made from the partly rotted, squashed remains of plants, can preserve skin, hair and clothing for thousands of years. When tests were carried out on the man's body they showed that it was around 2,000 years old. He was a Celt.

This Celt died in a very strange way. First, he was hit on the head and knocked out and then he was strangled with a knotted cord and stabbed in the throat. Finally, he was thrown face down into a pool in the bog. This suggests that the man was a sacrifice. He had been thrown into water, just like the metalwork offered to the gods.

DRUIDS
The Celts' sacrifices were performed by priests called Druids. Pliny, a Roman writer, said that the Druids used mistletoe in their ceremonies. Mistletoe pollen was found in the stomach of the Lindow man. He had probably been given it mixed in a drink, shortly before he was killed.

THE ROMAN INVASION

The Celtic way of life in southern Britain was shattered in AD 43. In that year, a Roman army crossed the English Channel.

Some of the southern tribes welcomed the invaders. Others fought fiercely, but they could not beat the Romans, who were much better organised. One by one, the Celtic hill-forts were captured and the tribes surrendered.

Key

Areas where Welsh spoken

Areas where Gaelic spoken

Roman rule brought big changes to Britain. The Romans built the first roads and proper towns in the country. They brought new styles of dress, a new language and a new religion, too. They stamped out the Druids and banned human sacrifice.

N

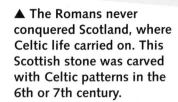

▲ The Romans never conquered Scotland, where Celtic life carried on. This Scottish stone was carved with Celtic patterns in the 6th or 7th century.

Welsh, a Celtic language, survives alongside English.

The Romans were the first of a series of foreign peoples who settled in Britain. They were followed by the Anglo-Saxons, the Vikings and the Normans. Over hundreds of years, people who spoke Celtic languages were pushed into the west and north. Despite everything, the old Celtic languages survived. Today, 650,000 people speak Welsh and 70,000 people speak Scottish Gaelic.

Until this century, many Scottish farmers lived in a type of house called a tigh dubh, or black house. It was built with the same methods used by the ancient Celts.

If you want to see the influence of the Celts, just look at a map of Britain. Place-names in Scotland, Wales and Cornwall are mostly Celtic. Almost all English rivers still have Celtic names. Avon and Tyne, for example, are both Celtic words, meaning 'river'.

GLOSSARY

broch
a stone tower-house, found in the north of Scotland

bronze
a metal made from tin and copper, and harder than both. Prized by the Celts for mirrors, shields and other decorative metalwork

chariot
a horse-drawn vehicle with two wheels, usually used in battle

crannog
a small artificial island found in many Scottish lochs. It had a house on top and was usually joined to the shore by a wooden walkway

Druid
a Celtic priest. Druids performed religious ceremonies, and they were believed to be able to look into the future

fogou
a Cornish underground passage, lined and roofed with stone slabs

furrow
a narrow trench made by a plough

hill-fort
a settlement on a hilltop, defended by earth banks and ditches

iron
a metal, much harder than bronze, used for tools and weapons. The Celts were the first British people to use iron, and so the Celtic period is often called the 'Iron Age'

lynchet
an earth ridge or bank, formed by ploughing on hillsides

noble
a rich and powerful person

sacrifice
an offering made to a god. People, animals and precious objects could all be sacrifices

tribe
a group of families living together and being ruled by a chief

wattle
twigs or branches woven together to make a wall

Timeline

c2000BC	British people begin to use bronze. The start of the 'Bronze Age'.
c1000BC	Bronze valuables, such as swords, begin to be placed in rivers, lakes and springs.
c800-700BC	British tribes begin to use iron. The start of the 'Iron Age'.
c700-500BC	Hill-forts built all over Britain.
c600BC	White Horse cut in the chalk at Uffington.
c100BC	Southern British tribes begin to use coins.
c80BC	Southern British tribes begin to make pottery using a wheel.
c100BC-AD50	'Lindow Man' killed.
55-54BC	Romans, led by Julius Caesar, make two expeditions to Britain.
AD43	Roman conquest of Britain begins.

PLACES TO VISIT

The British Museum, Great Russell St, London, WC1B 3DG: Includes the best collection of Celtic metalwork and the body found in the Lindow bog.

Butser Ancient Farm, near Chalton, Hampshire: A reconstruction of a Celtic farmstead which is also a working farm.

Chiltern Open Air Museum, Newlands Park, Gorelands Lane, Chalfont St Giles, Buckinghamshire, HP8 4AD: Includes a reconstruction of a Celtic round-house.

Colchester Museum, The Castle, Colchester, Essex, CO1 1TJ: Displays the treasures found in the Lexden grave-mound.

Iceni Village and Museum, Cockley Clay, Swaffham, Norfolk: A reconstructed settlement of the local tribe, the Iceni.

Maiden Castle, Winterborne St Martin, Dorset: One of the biggest hill-forts in the country.

Museum of the Iron Age, 6 Church Close, Andover, Hampshire, SP10 1DP: Includes finds from the nearby Danebury hill-fort, and reconstructions of life there. Visit the museum and then look at the hill-fort.

Museum of London, London Wall, London, EC2Y 5HN: Celtic metalwork found in the Thames.

Scottish Crannog Centre, Kenmore, Tayside, Scotland: A reconstruction of a crannog, with a visitors' centre displaying finds from the crannogs in the loch.

Welsh Folk Museum, St Fagans, Cardiff, CF5 6XB: Includes a Celtic village, with three round-houses.

INDEX